A Curious Shipwreck

A Curious Shipwreck

STEVE SPENCE

Shearsman Books
Exeter

First published in the United Kingdom in 2010 by
Shearsman Books Ltd
58 Velwell Road
Exeter EX4 4LD

www.shearsman.com

ISBN 978-1-84861-097-2
First Edition

Cover by Peter Rozycki

Acknowledgements
Some of these poems have previously appeared in the following
magazines and websites:
*Envoi, Fire, Global Tapestry, Great Works, The Journal, The Rialto,
Shearsman, Stride, Tears in the Fence, 10th Muse, The Text, Tremblestone*
and in the anthology *In the Presence of Sharks*,
edited by Ian Robinson and Norman Jope.

CONTENTS

for May Spence

and in memory of Stan Spence, 1918–2002

A wreck is a human tragedy & nature shows no mercy

Last night nobody came so I slipped into
a two-piece costume & accompanied
the pirate to his ship. Efficiency & equality
are not always happy bedfellows yet
there's mounting evidence that fish are
more intelligent than people give them
credit for being. Instead of physical
adventures, her mind wandered through
a maze of daydreams. As I approached
the shape, it crouched down & became
smaller. Perhaps we have to become
more sophisticated in our approach to
the visual image. As he spelt out the link
between the men in boots & the men in
suits, I walked back rapidly to the compound,
waving as I passed the orang-utan.

Claustrophobia reigns over the elegant,
marbled corridors as a gentle trickle of
allegation & innuendo threatens to become
a torrent. She started to say something but
then turned & climbed the stairs, looking
back at me over her shoulder for the
first few steps. For centuries, our island
nation has been seafaring & roaming,
hedonistic & insatiable, curiously mercantile
& unable to stay put. Why is it then, that so
many pirates find it difficult to express
themselves in what they wear? In anticipation,
the old tar cleaned the hilt of his cutlass &
loosened the blade in its sheath. Yet he
stopped himself, suddenly realising that a
plot revelation was spiralling out of control.

As well as getting a picture of the man I
planned to meet, I discovered much more
while I was on his trail. "He has come to me,
the silent boatman, to ferry me across the
wine-dark sea". This was not an encouraging

opening to a conversation but whatever
happened to the Bard of Salford? She was
on her knees, pressed against me, & the
carriage was swaying like a ship. Increasingly,
I find myself adopting unnatural positions in
order to move about at all. Her recovery sparked
a period of frantic literary activity & several books
were published which offered practical help with
navigation. Choosing what you want in life is an
art best guided from the heart but many of the
overweight pirates still refuse the offer of therapy.

At that moment a breath of wind parted the curtains

There was a mocking smile on her bloated
face which seemed to send him mad. Driven
by the imperatives of commerce, most
contemporary movies are little more than
products. Small groups of men move about
silently, yet there is no index of scale, no
reassuring hint of time or place. "Just look at
you, I had no idea you were such a fan of
the mollusc". Due to the credit crunch, city
financiers are facing a crackdown on expenses
yet they also believe that we've lost the ancient
world's respect for the night. So, the set was a
fantasy but what about the story? We'll pursue
the pirates as long as we have food & water.
There may be no place like home but we always
wander around thinking that there could be.

All these years in the wilderness & what have
we accomplished? Supporters range from
cocktail-sipping socialists to headscarved old
buccaneers in coastal retirement villages. Is
anxiety about sleep keeping us all awake? Yet
there's so much to do that you'll never run out
of inspiration & things to try. A friend once told
me that he felt like a ghost in his own life but
he picks up the bill for breakfast as if it's a
perfectly normal thing to do. Much depends on
the quality of the apples. I'm not sure if they
were pirates but they wore high boots & had
long black hair & heavy black moustaches.
At that moment a breath of wind parted the
curtains & I moved across the room to
the window.

There is no relief in sight for those hankering
after the model's life but when did pathologists
start looking like Tara Fitzgerald? Argentina
is reaping the soya while the sun shines. From
below deck she produced a bottle of cabernet

& we both had a glass. Because of their large
beaks, pirates are reckoned to be ferocious
adversaries, although there is a tendency for
humankind to see itself as being somehow
apart from the natural world. What does it mean
to control a business where stocks are low & prices
high? My breathing slowly returned to normal along
with my heart rate. There is surely no cause for
alarm but he had an excessive, almost hysterical
attention to detail. Undeterred, they avoided
capture & returned to their piratical careers.

Let's consider other people's words & how we misuse them

Many are the actors & pirates who
rely on others putting words into their
mouths. Here already is the rich
aromatic breath of resins, a presage
of the smell of pinewoods & summer
days. Yet how could such a tiny,
wingless creature reach the empty
island so quickly? Perhaps the difference
is merely a matter of tone yet pirates
are crippling themselves with impact
exercises. Although salt is very much
derided these days, we still have a
deep desire & craving for something
fishy. Interest is fixed for twelve months,
calculated daily on the cleared balance
& paid at maturity.

One thing is certain: offering steady
employment with benefits & holiday pay
is a practice which has fallen out of
economic fashion. With hits like *Don't
you want me, baby,* The Human League
took an art agenda onto the high street.
There were bottles flying everywhere but
the pirates simply decided to carry on
with their performance. Waterspouts
pick up fish & transport them live to
nearby lakes & streams. It's a good thing
we don't have to apply these rules to
potential lovers. There is some evidence
that this process is underway yet today you
can sail close by the islands without ever
guessing their violent history.

Fish, to the Mesopotamians, were majestic
creatures, yet it's time to step off the scale
& get out the tape measure. What has
prompted France's youth to turn from sensible

tipplers into full-time abusers? For their
part, the factory owners are in no rush to
expand the size of their workforce, so you
really get the flavours dancing in your mouth.
Pirates don't come to enjoy the floats & the
music, they come to commit acts of violence.
Let's consider other people's words & how
we misuse them. More to the point, aren't
our campuses supposed to be overflowing
with troublemaking, tenured radicals? Yet
every sea has its own characteristic which
contributes to the texture of pirate society.

But it's not file-sharing, it's piracy . . .

Faint shuffling sounds reached us now &
then & an occasional hollow beating of
wings. Should you call your children
George & Emma or plump for Storm &
Savannah? For most of the summer, the
issue was pushed to the background by
other events yet the pirates were off the
leash & on the lash. Silver hit the water
sideways, broke a leg & was still on
crutches a year later. As the pirate turned
towards me I noticed a small blemish on
her left shoulder. I didn't think anything
worse could happen but as I reeled away
I saw a sight even more terrifying. As with
all markets, the basic forces of supply &
demand are in operation.

For the first few months I visited him, he
seemed cheerful & sanguine, despite
sleeping in a room with three pirates of
hideous appearance & terrifying habits.
London has become a tropical lagoon
filled with weird & wonderful creatures.
Yet the Tudor-bowl haircut has been
gaining a disturbing momentum among
male models & hipsters. He was exhausted,
his muscles ached & his back & arms were
bruised, but the old tar became quiet again,
his brief escapade forgotten. There is
something melancholy about the sea wrestling
back land we have made our own. In twenty
years we may be looking at jellyfish & chips
rather than fish & chips.

It's been suggested that alcohol stimulates
the striatum, an area of the brain important
in sexual attraction. What kind of meaningful
democracy can emerge from such a thought?
Alice knew little about pirates yet her education

left her with a skewed & slightly unlikely mix
of knowledge. Higher energy prices translate
into higher food prices & higher food prices
tend to create serious political discontent.
She had a knack for stating the obvious yet
some of the pirates glanced back & made
vague protective gestures. Marinade is
the noun & marinate the verb: pirates often
get this wrong but after a drink everyone
looks more desirable. In a few moments
Silver slowly rose & shook himself.

Solutions, whole or partial, are not entirely lacking

There was screaming in the background,
then the radar went silent. Tell him if he
doesn't find water soon, he's going to
drown. Previously a good student, she
was suspended twice for cheating. There
were fears last night that the problem could
spread south of the border. I was in a fairly
large cabin, furnished with dark wood, sofas
& brass fittings, yet the rivals never failed to
come to blows. How I wish I'd lurked outside
the polling-station with an anti-Boris banner.
Focus in on a cone-snail & make a friend for
life. Do films about changing the world ever
make any money? Mass executions of pirates
are often staged to deter others yet boredom
is just what we need.

It was growing towards dusk & the autumn
light was setting in but we recommend Devil's
Nest, a scrambling of avocado, sour cream &
spicy sausage. Body armour & helmets are
either worn or within reach at all times. She was
not her usual sweet self & she bit me in three
places. From out of nowhere, a speedboat came
alongside the tanker & opened fire with machine-
guns & rocket-propelled grenades. Then they
both bowed low & their curls became hopelessly
entangled. A ship is a small world. To the best of
my knowledge, Heathcote Williams has never
appeared in a film about pirates yet I knew I had
to go my own way, that it was better for me to be
alone. The fish-footman began by producing
an enormous package from under his arm.

From time to time, there's an agitation to crack
down on pirates yet the threat of a bite is far more
effective than the actual bite. What's a trademark
worth? She pressed her hand softly over her belly
& her smile broadened. On the contrary, nobody

wants to be bored but Groucho Marx's solution
was to ring people up in the middle of the night
& shout at them. Suddenly, men's skin-deep
beauty has become their unique selling-point,
while librarians are obsessive classifiers who
impose on chaos an order they know to be fiction.
How do we get down to the beach? There is a
lofty ambition at work here. Alice led the way & the
whole party swam to the shore in unison. In the
privacy of his own home he expressed himself
through the medium of creative dance.

Pirates

After considering the known facts the green pirate opted for the Sargasso Sea. Strange mutating snake-things inhabited the area. They were mainly bright green, similar to the pirate's emerald hue but they glowed with uncanny quickness, electric deep in an awkward kind of way. They bothered no-one but trouble was in sure for sureness. "Too many adjectives", said the pirate. "This is not the sort of story I want to belong to".

Pirate the yellow operated in a different thought zone altogether. After blanketing out the QWERTYUIOPETCETERA of his 1920's model he pondered the non-evolution of the keyboard motel. Need a holiday, he thought, trying hard to think himself back into a REAL narrative but it was already too late in the afternoon of his discontent and post-modernism had been and GONG eloquently resuscitating its hermaphrodite nature along the way. Brother Blue will help me out here, he cogitated thoughtlessly, unaware of the inherent contradiction of this statement.

Blue was also thoughtless, plundering the horse's mane with an Irish contingent of wordless buccaneers. "Action is allness, words is nowt,"—a hearty truism he took in with his mother's milk. Except, of course, he had no mother, being made instantly upon the conjunction of a full stop and an artless colon wherein their feckless copulatory impulse rendered him alive and full of pain. Kicking against the pricks, he thought to himself. Time for Red to set the record straight.

Redness was a condition of great anxiety to the fourth pirate, the one most readily available to the kiddywinks after too much RE and a double dose of MATHEMATICS. Fearful stuff, I remember it well. Despite such an almighty setback, he sailed the seven seas of cod liver oil, warming his frozen hands in times of need at the brightness of his name's content and vigorously pumping iron. "These cannonballs are all too ominous", he joked lugubriously. "Time to head for land I think and Black ought to take a turn at the wheel".

Black was rightly named, unlike the others, whose apparel was not suited to their titles. He was adorned from head to feet in a not-a-colour negative, an escapee from left-bank modishness, mean as a lemon shark and tastily neutral in matters of the heart. He sailed alone, bar a retinue of robots who variously cooked his food—always burnt to a cindery blackness—unfurled the sails and navigated abroad but he was a nefarious loner who preferred the blankness of his own company to the chattery impulses of the other pirates. There is no story here, merely an endless attempt to put one word in front of another, but Black was unconcerned. He was semantically illiterate and all the better for it.

Purple. The concluding mariner. Likes to be seen in the company of lewd women and convivial to a turn. Taciturn but gregarious. Lets his sword hand do the talking. Lets his crewmen do the plundering. Keeps himself in reserve for the finer arts of conversing with brevity and copulating with copious. His favourite food being baked bean sarnies and always to be found at the breadbin of life. After twenty years at sea, he's returned to the orchards where he can be seen re-enacting the piratical certitudes for a new generation of schoolkids in a virtual-reality scenario which beats the pants off working for a living. What more can there be to say?

Dissolving Textures

"You sir, are a rogue & a liar: the trout
in Beefheart's *replica* is, in fact, a carp."

Would you call me a cynic, Jane?
It was here that evaluation became
most difficult. Although they'd known
each other for six months, they found
they could still surprise themselves in
various ways.

The process of social discipline was not
as yet disconnected. Jack Tarr is behind
the bar on Sunday morning when I walk in.
The place smells of cooking—bacon &
eggs. At such a moment, hunters gather
in astonishing numbers. The Methodist
tradition here is mostly ambivalent.
What could that mean? You will not
like me. "God", Marissa interjected.
"You look like your jaw is unhinged".

Pete was getting that funny look again,
the one I was becoming familiar with.
I was starting to feel a sort of vicarious
pleasure related to his new-found
celebrity. The gentlemen will be
envious & the ladies will be repelled.

Without women, Helen realised, men
do strange things. "Your mate", she said.
"That's not *him*, is it?" If you were here
more often you'd realise that we all sink
into an abyss. An elegy to prey & predator.

A curious & most puzzling question might
be stated concerning the visual matter as
touching the Leviathan. "Yeah, that's Pete",
I said, & turned to him as if to establish
our friendship & also his identity.

In Xanadu, did Kubla Khan?
Such examples, pluckt from scores readily
to hand, may convey the flavour of puns
& wordplay & I'll love it. She made a noise
deep in her throat & the lava began to rise.
"A whale did that?" A whale as big as an island.

Valuable food like this will not go to
waste in the ocean. He took a deep
breath & unhooked it, carefully, reverentially.
He smiled uncertainly & sidled out of
the shop in suitably enigmatic fashion.

The point of this game was to preserve
the excitement of novelty. Air guitar player
wanted. Must be fit & possess own instrument.

If you consider the buccaneer from this
standpoint, it will be clear to us why he
suffered so much under his ludicrous
dual personality. In an hour she was gone,
assuring me that it would go better next time.

Dwarfed by the vast expanse of open ocean,
he called every night & told her how much he
missed her, the biggest animal that ever lived
on our planet, how he liked her & just felt so
natural & comfortable with her.

Yet the ocean never rests. Huge currents
such as the gulf-stream keep its waters
constantly on the move around the globe.
Here the Methodist tradition is ambivalent.
On the one hand, we sprawled in the boat,
our legs intertwined, & rubbed suntan lotion
into each others' skin. Wet, drenched through
& shivering cold, Methodist preachers
perfected techniques to arouse paroxysms
of fear & death.

At night, strapped to our masts,
we listen to the wailing sirens.
& you'll wonder who that could have
been if not Pirate Jenny. The sheer
quantity of marine life the sea
contains far exceeds that of the land.

swashbucklers

any passing ranter will do
but where was a cop
when you needed one
amuse yourself
while awaiting events
orange—pay as you go
directly or on-line
picking crab apples
in fox's wood
chased as a poacher
by bailiff & dogs
'left the trout in the river'
city boy at heart
tho' a stream & a few trees
wouldn't go amiss
arboretum johnny
don't go near a nunnery
not yet awhile at any rate
exchange value of
intellectual property
resist all transaction
bill gates wins the day
again
& it's a glorious summer
of our discs for rent
swam awhile at devil's point
chased by a demon
frankie drake's a privateer
legalised pirate more like
tautology
call a spade a garden fork

never miss a trick
pressed by a gang of four
to cut a demo in favour
of the misshapen &
disadvantaged boys
broke the bank
walked the dog
drank the beer
quaffed it down
ran away for christmas
fell down in tears
started to read moby
again
not a buccaneer in sight
tulip bulbs are toxic
read it somewhere in a book
thank you roger jolly
moon the loon
all that inarticulate longing
won't get fooled again i said
hummed & harred 'bout it
juliette lewis & the licks
joker in the pack
posh englishman i'm not
derek is eric
& keith is johnny's dad
i'm not from luton she said
i'm from inner space instead
alexander selkirk was real
but also a fictional being
not a *real* real pirate
real pirates are
economic globalists
knew that for ever

Pirates in Rock

The Shamrock Pirates

Pete & the Pirates

The Shy Pirates

The Angry Pirates

Dead Smiling Pirates

The Edelweiss Pirates

The Bilge Pumps

Jolly Rogers

Brine & Bastards

The Crimson Pirates

The Pirate Jennies

Adam & the Ants

Rusty Cutlass

The Whisky Bards

The Sky Pirates

The Brigands

The Bounding Main

Johnny Kidd & the Pirates

Rock Pirates

Nylon Pirate

The Dayglo Pirates

At World's End

Trudging back, through the tears
of my nausea, I saw him moving
up the incline towards me. It was
a time for robust gadgets. The
language of piracy is rootless,
irresponsible and motivated by
base desires. As we sit here we
are all being slightly squeezed
and stretched. There is, of course,
a variety of inferior 'meats' on sale:
red herrings and bloaters, cow-heel,
sheep's trotters, pig's ear, faggots,
tripe and black pudding. Poison is
Queen!

As the frenzy continues, walls of
bubbles drift upwards. I am not
an aficionado of the grape, Clive.
She was searching all the time,
searching for interesting people.
Due to the peace spreading across
Europe, many sailors and privateers
found themselves underemployed.
Out in the open ocean, unimpeded
by land, such swells can become
gigantic. She didn't see me at all,
but I'll bet a month hasn't gone by
since, that I haven't thought of that
girl. A merry life and a short one!

Meat, like wheat, involves feelings
of status over & above its dietary
value. It's difficult to find really
interesting people. Surely the riddle is
on the point of being solved.? Burning
houses, breaking hedges, treading
down corn: such were the means by

which the poor retaliated against
their betters. Then suddenly the
realization: that the pirate's belt was
so old, that he had always worn it,
struck her with a strange, sharp
pain. Something lurches deep
within the girl who was death!

How does the graviton relate to
gravitational waves? A single-
sentence answer is required.
The typhoon analogy suggests
that high unemployment and
record inflation just blow up like
a storm. I know, but she keeps
searching. Cursing was a means
by which the weak and defenceless
tried to avenge themselves upon
their enemies. Shell the eggs and
prick them all over with a fork, rub
them with a little garam masala
& set them aside. For this ceremony
we demand coquetry & particular
clothes. We're talking very seriously
here about things which might not
actually exist!

He was beautiful! He swaggered onto
the ship like a pirate, mesmerised the
crew and then split. On his approach,
she fell on her knees & embraced
his feet, with looks full of gratitude &
love. The term 'deity' is, in any useful
sense, meaningless. It's the weekends
that have done the damage—the years
have been kind to you. It is now
midsummer & the sun is shining at full
strength. The jargon of every trade or
calling is gradually borrowed by others,

to add to their stock of metaphor. You
are without doubt, the worst pirate I've
ever heard of!

There was a girl waiting to get on the
ferry. Do you like rainbows? She was
carrying a white parasol. Can you hum
the tune of *Puff the Magic Dragon?*
I only saw her for a second. Are you
partial to a bit of barefoot walking?
Gravity is the least-understood force
in the universe yet much of his uneasiness
was now removed. He had a friend to
whom he could impart his thoughts,
and whose experience could assist him
in his designs. At sea one day, you'll
see land where there is no land.
Exit offstage, pursued by a bear!

"Not much mistake about that,"
said Spanker. Pale & still as death,
the two fugitives huddled in the boat
amid sounds of gunfire & hand-to-hand
fighting. "Sharks get very excited when
pirates are around." China's red-hot
economy is likely to enjoy at least two
more years of double-digit growth as its
gravitational pull creates the daily
advances and retreats of the tide.
The mechanics of buying gives way to
a complete eroticization of choosing &
spending. Caught by the backlash,
the Banshees made a public apology
for their previous actions. Even boiling
a kettle, it seems, is a piratical act!

These are the most productive seas
on earth. One moment we were both

groping downstairs, leaving the candle
by the empty chest, and the next we
had opened the door and were in full
retreat. There's more to life than
reading the news. Here was a stirring
of revolt in the heart of a sincere man,
whose grief had been disturbed by
exaggeration & lust. There is a sort
of doily etiquette which reminds the
diligent reader of shoe-fetishism in
film studies. "The name's Neff, two
f's, as in Philadelphia!"

This emphasis on death &
destruction set the pace for what
followed, as Spanker's preening
dandyism hit the spot. Light waves
clearly travel through a vacuum.
Fry the remaining onions & use
them to garnish the pilau. Stella
& I both awake early & decide
to have breakfast together.
Sprinkle the cashew nuts &
coconut over the top & serve
with pickle or chutney. Light
radiates from a huge pearly white
structure which is oriental in design.
Yet another legend speaks of a
magic potion containing the
excrement of a toad. "You know,
you ought to find yourself a girl!"

Everything was driven by her
desire at all costs to avoid
another deficit. Are we going to
have a heat-wave this summer?
A poem & a pirate with a message
enters his consciousness as the
threat of bombing makes sleeping

a more complex and public affair.
The creature trots towards him
on the empty street, with something
struggling in its mouth. Spanker drops
to his knees & the parrot speaks
with great rapidity: "Pieces of eight!
Pieces of eight! Pieces of eight!"

English punk was now open to
every charlatan, poseur & pirate
attracted by the profits of media
attention & a record contract.
Be careful not to overheat the oil
as this will make the whites puffy
and brown. It was a good day for
city analysts. "You're an unusual
kind of pirate. What's your name?"
It's very moving and emotional
that people feel this strong
connection with Captain Jack.
"I am the manager of the Café
Corsair & I will tell you things
at random!"

Falling asleep & inducing the
right sleep have become key
components in the market-driven
economy. It is now easier to follow
Venus into daylight than find her
later in the day, as we can estimate
her position in relation to nearby
landmarks. In a few minutes, mother
and daughter were safely ensconced
in the cave, while I sat peering
through the narrow entrance,
waiting for dawn to break.
Spanker, meanwhile, desired only
to be rich & to conceal his riches
from the other pirates!

Something to declare

This film has everything, a beautiful
actress, a tragic shipwreck & a
lost fortune, yet some fear that
its failure will bring the financial
system to its knees. As I ambled
out of the door, cruelly cool & whistling,
she started to cry. It's a little
masterpiece of elegance &
economy, irony & dirty-mindedness.

"Some of these worms are
extremely successful", said Dr.
Livesy. After a tiring day among
the wildlife you need a base to
return to for some pampering.
As for Captain Teach, he had
long signalled his intention to
stand down in the hope of
keeping his enemies at bay.

It's rare to meet a genius at any
point in one's life yet whenever
he came into the room you could
immediately feel the temperature
rise. When a mood of excitement
surrounds a market, all sensible
people circle the wagons. This is
the kind of rank hypocrisy which
gives pirates & piracy a bad name.

& the pirates look into the abyss

Pirates communicate with each
other by transmitting & receiving
snatches of sound yet they
meddle in the markets at their
peril. Delivery is completely
free with no minimum order value
& our prices are very reasonable.
This operation is a warning to all
those engaged in criminal activity.

When the revolution came, it was
a revolution of the market. It's as
though he dropped anchor in the
middle of the continent simply in
order to write about the sea.
Such bouts of socialising raise
the possibility that this particular
group of seamen are related. All
pirates are on the minimum wage.

There are many reasons for the
loss of pirate schools but it can
surely be put down to a general
decline in cultural sensibility.
Most of his work is dense with
meaning but the corpse looked on
with uncomprehending admiration.
An elegant feeding ballet is set to
the pirate's own music.

All you need is a sexy trolley with big wheels

"Have you ever had a sardine
smoothie?", asked Alice. Yet
the point about the pirates is
that they were on the margins
of polite society. Over time,
gold will never lose its value.
Meanwhile, back on Planet
Earth, let us consider the
other end of the spectrum.

"Are you still as drunk as a
pike, stewed as a barbel,
soused as a mackerel,
chinned as a chub, razzled
as a roach, grilled as a
gudgeon, pickled as a perch,
pooped as a pollack, trockled
as a trout, dizzied as a dace &
boozed-up as a gilt-head bream?"

As before the group settled
down & paid us little attention.
Yet my back felt parched & I
was dizzy from the heat &
brightness. After lunch the
pirates swam back to the beach
& lay down on their oversize
pink towels. British pirates are
fearless in the face of derision.

It's a sombre picture & one that chills the blood

No one can honestly predict
what's going to happen during
the next few weeks. Pirates tend
to be creative types, brimming
with ideas & ready to learn
through trial & error. "But I dislike
intoxicating fluids, I prefer the
bitter truth", said Alice, who just
wanted to set all the mad people free.

Will the pirates thrive or crumble
as the global economy crashes
all around us? Alice sat blowing
perfect smoke rings, a skill she
learned aboard the pirate ship.
Nobody knew what changed the
captain's mind but he was a man
of charm, who talked well & fluently,
with imagination & humour.

"Bearded, muscular & prone to
grunting—I think I like the sound
of prehistoric pirates!" Drink was
mostly taken in moderation yet
the whole process seemed so
mysterious that one hardly knew
how to begin thinking about it.
English pirates have a long history
of relishing the rabbit.

Mission impossible

Quite how the crisis will be
resolved is unclear yet
eventually you simply slide
into a trance, barely aware
of your own existence. Don't
breathe a word about this to
anybody. It's important to retain
some perspective as we enter
these confusing new times.

Henry Morgan, Anne Bonney,
Mary Read, Edward Teach,
Charles Vane, Stede Bonnet,
Francis Drake & John Hawkins.
"Now, if you had to chose only
one of these eight pirates to take
with you to your desert island,
which one would it be?" There
was no place left to go.

Five minutes later the pirate was
lounging in Alice's living room
with a glass of rum perched on
his knee. "I'm encouraged by the
linguistic signifiers you hide behind",
he said. Cruelly sharp fingers raked
his face, yet they spent most of
their time arguing about whether
Wagner was better than Punk.

Reasons to be cheerful

As my sickness returned I was
absorbed by a gloomy black
melancholy that nothing could
dissipate. Yet Alice's spirits
were high & she bounded
along with feelings of unbridled
joy & hilarity. Is the credit crunch
going to lead us deeper into
the climate crunch?

There are very few pirates who
actually admit they enjoy writing
yet you have to be a consumer;
if you don't buy lots of stuff you're
not a good citizen. Paranoia is
far more common than had been
expected & is also on the increase.
"The truth is", said Alice, "you are
rather difficult to fathom".

Some pirates come for the cocktails,
cuisine & designer chic yet he was
a meat-&-two-veg kind of guy who
liked his gravy as thick as treacle.
As a source of light, the mirror
enjoys a special place in the room.
"Coming off the booze", he said,
"is like being jilted by the love of
your life".

Readers become writers

Consumption is irrepressible
because it's founded on lack.
You wouldn't have thought
there was enough money in the
world to buy all the goods on
sale in Hong Kong. Yet everyone
was waiting for noon & the three
hour siesta. The pirate turned
away & looked out to sea.

Once unmasked, the pirate
either collapses or takes refuge
in another tale. Like most dreams,
advertising is devoid of all negativity
& relativity. Yet do we really need
to believe in our own propaganda?
In their final bedroom scene, the
pirates progress from spontaneous
affection to growing alienation.

With the close-up, space expands,
with slow-motion, movement is
extended. There is no simple
relationship between kinds of ship
& kinds of pirate. Alice scowled, like
a puritan lured to a party, & then
wrote the word PIRATE on his face.
Let us grant that our everyday objects
are, in fact, objects of passion.

& we'll plunge into the deep

An expression of terror briefly
crossed his face & he darted
her a glance of extreme
curiosity. "Are you dreaming
of the sea again", asked Alice.
At length, the pirate arose,
took a candle from the table
& proceeded to seat himself
on the old sea chest. It was
all in a day's routine.

Let us imagine a lone sailor,
struggling in the darkness to
keep his little boat afloat. Oh,
to live in a civilisation that
doesn't need alarm clocks!
For the most part, of course,
the sailor's life is an uneventful
one, but what we have here
is a Tower of Babel, for each
pirate speaks in his own idiom.

In the world of the pirates the
past & the exotic each has a
social dimension. If you look
carefully you might just find a
beach to yourself. Yes, but it's
going to be a blustery day with
showers. "If we lose the bees,
we lose everything", said Alice,
then showed the pirates how to
cook an authentic fish pickle.

In pursuit of the pirates

It may sound idyllic but the island
was already haunted by a famous
pirate, raucously shouting "shiver
me timbers", I shouldn't wonder.
I once watched a pig, from the
window of my flat, in the middle
of the night, during a thunderstorm,
& it was digging a long furrow—for
worms or truffles, you may well ask!

This year autumn felt like it had
started way back in the middle of
august, yet I love the noise of the
sea, probably the most relaxing
sound there is. At night, creatures
from the deep visit the surface while
the price of a work of art has now
become part of its function, "How
do we put this ship back together?"

As Alice fastened the boat, an
albatross flew very low & caught
her on the shoulder with its wing.
Much worse was still to come yet
the pirates' actions, as well as their
attire, single them out as abnormal
heroes. As usual, the little people
will be paying for the mess made
by the men in big trousers.

Perhaps with a dash of panache?

Which is the more urgent task,
saving the planet or rescuing the
city? Yet recent research suggests
a probable biological basis for a
person's political outlook. As the
reluctant pirate is sucked into the
maelstrom, he needs to summon
all his resolve to save the crew
from drowning.

You may choose to start the day
with breakfast alfresco or end it
with a moonlit dinner a deux, yet
in the erotic life of men & women
there is no such thing as health.
Easy-going, talkative male, witty,
honest, respectable, seeks similar
lady, 30–50, for great friendship &
acts of piracy.

Remarkably little is known about
the extent of home education in
the United Kingdom, yet where
else in the world can you visit
a museum dedicated to shoes?
Pirates mostly bond by doing things
that involve standing & looking in
the same direction together. Suddenly,
the ocean is alive with cetaceans.

Uncovering the secrets of great pirate migrations

What is consciousness &
what is it for? "As a further
precaution, I think you ought
to shave off your beard", said
Alice. Her cheeks were ruddy
& her black eyes bright with
mischief, yet the very idea of
celebrity was anathema to the
pirate. Can jellyfish sing & if
so how do their brains light up?

Are you a lazy alto when you
could be a soprano if you tried?
Pirates, like taxi-drivers, usually
have great spatial memories.
That evening, Alice felt more
reluctant than usual to leave the
ship, yet the hourly rate for piracy
hasn't increased since the 1970's.
To be a poet & a parrot seems
eccentric, even slightly perverse.

Haunted by the ideas & styles
of the past, we felt there was no
space in which to operate. If
you're going fishing you need to
buy some hooks. For the first
time in his life his optimism failed
him yet Alice's humour was of
the unsettling variety, which
made it necessary to examine
his own received ideas.

But it looks like a bird built by a surrealist

Alice was cooking a red mullet
when it suddenly went up in flames.
Amid all the incidents of piracy this
has to be the most unusual. Our
civilization has more & more objects
& fewer & fewer names for them.
Yet the pirate started work on a
peacock worm which he found at
low tide. It's only when a familiar
pattern is built up that confidence
is restored.

It's important for pirates to be
conservationists as they're so
much a part of the landscape.
Yet there were no paths in the
forest & they were soon completely
lost. The bearded pirate is
companionable & calm by nature,
making him the ideal pet for
young children. In the bedroom,
their hard-edged glamour is
combined with a shabby chic style.

When pirates can be recognised
by their beards alone, it's a sure
sign that they've achieved cult
status. "Yes, but can you resist
the hog's pudding with honey-
roasted apples?" asked Alice.
No sooner did she recover from
one mishap than another disaster
struck. America couldn't wait to
see the back of Bush & Cheney
& neither could the pirates.

The unseen behind the seen

Taking a walk for pleasure was
an incomprehensible notion for
the pirates. They were rock 'n'
roll outlaws even if they were
packaged as a television show,
Scars are thought to be a symbol
of masculinity according to recent
research. Her laughter was loud
& derisive. Without a horizon you
don't know where you are.

There was something about her
he never fathomed, an aloofness,
a mystery drawing him powerfully
to her. "What about busking in
other parts of the world?" asked
Alice. Pour the chutney into hot,
sterilised jars & cover with vinegar-
proof paper. "I'm simply nuts about
vinegars, all of them", said Alice.
He never tired of learning from women.

A cold front will bring rain to all
pirates this afternoon. Is the
global credit crisis providing new
opportunities for the Mafia?
"The song that I'd like to pass on
to my children is a sea-shanty by
Sean McGowan", said Alice. In all
The books I've read the English are
always running away to sea, yet why
is gold suddenly back in fashion?

Piratica exotica

Alice brought in a wind-up
tape-recorder & taught the
pirates how to use it. She
was wearing the same black
dress but no earrings on this
occasion. Women seeking
short-term relationships find
buccaneering types with
facial scars more attractive.
The clock is to time as the
mirror is to space.

"Post-modernism has many
baroque characteristics",
said Alice. This sparked the
usual debates about the
mass-marketing of rebellion.
Even customers in credit are
having more taken from their
accounts, though pirates
aren't usually given to extreme
expressions of emotion, "You're
so in the loop", said Alice.

Have you ever come across
a misshapen parsnip that
looks like Esther Rantzen?
Serve with apple sauce, a
fruity chutney or something
like a Waldorf Salad. So, who's
attending these courses on
how to take direct action?
Finally, there is the question
of how the pirate mind
actually works.

Revolt into Style

(i.m. George Heywood Melly)

Anarchist,
pirate,
impresario,
rejuvenator
of trad. jazz,
art-historian,
partygoer,
bon-vivant
fly-fisherman,
auto-biographer
(warts 'n' all),
seasoned
raconteur,
film-reviewer,
music critic,
compulsive
storyteller,
surrealist,
wearer-of-suits
(flamboyant
dresser),
lover-of-life,
hopelessly
drunk on
everything
the world
had to offer,
good-time george,
(smelly melly),
wearer of the
eye-patch,
notorious boozer,
drunk-as-a-skunk,
lewd & loathsome
(say some),
cultured & civilised
(say his friends),

public school
extrovert,
fly-in-an-ointment
liverpudlian
(scouse mouse),
ordinary seaman
(of the skiving
variety),
george wasn't
officer material,
that's for sure!
not an introvert
bone in his body,
high on life &
sex & drugs &
rock & roll, yet
neurotically
fastidious,
refused all
honours under
new labour,
yet held four
honorary
degrees,
a reveller in
contradiction,
performer,
entertainer,
educator,
subversive,
broadcaster,
husband,
parent,
fan of bessie
smith, analyser
of pop culture,
leveller of class
(by his example),
freethinker,
libertine,

(not an
ovaltineey!),
blues singer
with a great
voice, an
irrepressible
wearer of hats—
his speciality
being the
fedora, avid
collector of
paintings,
film scriptwriter,
posh yet demotic,
unabashedly exotic,
on stage until the
end, an example
to us all.

On the Hoe

Exegesis or hermeneutics it's all the same to me
call it what you will between the teller of the tale
(tall story) & the he or she who reads what's written
black smudges on off-white newsprint maybe there's
an enormous chasm big enough to encompass
worlds (microcosm macrocosm) is this what we call
the imagination this interaction between minds miles
adrift & years (light) apart? when the stars threw
down their spears no I've heard that one before
somewhere got to keep the narrative afloat & full
of piracy however loopy the results marine life in
buckets crabs sea urchins speckled-fin tuna fish
guppies blennies reef 'cuda's cuckoo wrasses pixie-
winged plantins thick-lipped grouper fishes green
pollacks red mullets blue sunfish yellow canary sea
basses & antelope sea-horses crowded into sea-pink
plastic bucket worlds within something receding into
ever circling diminishers wordplay not my forte but
must avoid a full-stop at all costs imperative over &
out ROGER.

There's someone swimming in the sea I think it's
a poet or some similar exotic species a pirate
perhaps sam bellamy or it may be kenny knight
or captain kidd no it's seamus heaney now half a
million nicker richer we ought to invite him to read
at the language club and ask him for a contribution
to the next poetry anthology & other outstanding
businesses Surfing on (capital S for me or reader?)
the internet only the other day I came across this
strange missive crackling & fizzing for all it was
worth & attempting to pass itself off as a poem much
as I'm doing here with this biro bic hand job on the
back of an envelope.

michael heseltine (no caps small minded man)
purportedly wrote his career plan on such &
reckoned to be pm by his sixth decade screwed
that one up good & JOLLY well done michael

well done keep on wearing the eye patch &
keep up the good work I'm coming to the end.
eschatological finale I must go on I can't go on
I'll go on—sorry sam more plagiarism—I'll go on
never not won't will why when all in all it's only
ever always maybe a matter of interpretation Amen.

At first the pirates give him a hard time

We stop at a break in the
trees & begin dividing our
spoils as the spectre of
Adorno comes clean.

Think of the first really stupid
thing that comes into your
mind. Pirates have a high
opinion of the world's regard.

As the barking of a hundred
dogs sound in my ear,
scholars write learned articles
about Long John Silver.

Shortly after we set off, the
boats ran aground. The names
of the sirens are invariably
connected to speech.

Such policies are easy to design
but Humpty Dumpty has fallen
off his perch & there is no way of
putting him back together again.

Many of the pirates were more
experienced than I, yet ah!, what
memories an amoeba would have,
if it had any memories at all.

But here was another astonishing
fact: piracy had ruthlessly
thrust itself into the world & now
the world was coming to claim it.

For the moment nobody said a
word, yet still I did not realise how
mad she was & how accustomed
she was to screaming.

The problem of growth was
assumed to have been solved yet
he began talking to girls again, albeit
with overdue caution & unease.

Ready to pounce

All anomalies have a practical value.
Much the same can be said of
biological materials. Yet just suppose
I were to close my eyes & never open them again.

I've often thought that the people who
know all the answers are bound to be
much happier than those who don't.
A discovery is made which changes the way we think.

He wore a skull-cap & a wide shawl
of the richest silk around his body. On
tour, the pirates use fender mustangs
because of their trebly, scratchy sound.

To take the most obvious example, prices
cannot be allowed to fall to zero. But it's tomato
time again, so let's get stuck into the glut & lay
down a little summer sweetness for the autumn.

Our world is much closer to that of the pirates,
yet a young jellyfish is beautifully transparent
for all that. Many years of effort & billions of
pounds have been wasted putting men on the moon.

We shouldn't push the metaphor of
the island too far, but there, jutting
into the lagoon, is a platform with
insect-like figures moving on the deck.

He looked devilishly handsome, fair hair
falling over his face, his eyes a piercing
blue in the morning light. The pirates'
bodies were hanging limply from a tree.

By such slow teasing, he held her on the
edge of hysteria. Things only get crisp when
dissonance creeps in. Yet it was a great place
to hang out & meet like-minded bohemians.

Great claims are made for the
healing value of the royal touch
yet the patient workers, their eyes firmly
fixed upon the future, will quietly set things right.

It was an exciting & powerful gesture

When they were almost upon him,
he raised the pistol & fired. Placing
my hands on the top of the palisade,
I climbed over without difficulty.

His deep-sunk eyes peered up at
Jack as he came near. The tide had
turned but this was no ordinary tide
& the pirates returned to their foraging.

The challenge here is to survive
extreme change. He was more
interested in words than in objects.
Then came the clang of broken glass.

An obliging doctor bowed & silence
reigned. There were, he thinks, at
least seven or eight of the creatures.
An object bought on credit will still be mine.

Despite the change, the island
remained a libertarian idyll. The
audience were baffled but essentially
what we proposed was straightforward.

Obviously she enjoys dressing up
on even the slightest occasion. The
entire effect was deliberately alien
but you can't have it both ways.

At dinner last night I was offered
a menu with a multiple choice
of dishes. Thus an abundance of
advertising puts an end to insecurity.

It is said that privateers were the
licensed marauders of the sea.
In which case the status of a whole
civilisation changes overnight.

Her scorn was intolerable, yet
the rumours of war, it seemed,
were true. An abundance of
products puts an end to scarcity.

For three weeks they waited & not a sail did they see

Their revolt was instinctive & existential yet
she was no longer tempted to retrace her
steps & elude him. A bad temper is a great
asset to a sailor's bleak existence.

It was time for the pirates to recruit some
tough leaders, to check their gunpowder &
mass their forces. They were a ferocious set
of men with shaggy beards & scowling brows.

The shore was flanked with palm trees.
Ibiza's clubs had alfresco dance floors
lit up by the moon & the stars. Most of
the bouncers were ex-pirates.

Sure enough, they were there, a dozen or
so, big green fellows, with fine tapered bodies
& spotted wings. This was not merely an
abstract area of intellectual speculation, then?

The balcony swayed under him as he
stepped onto it & he still felt faint. ."Did
you enjoy the execution?", asked Peter,
with another attempt at conversation.

I was certain that we must part our ways
at once, that I must if necessary, put an
ocean between us. Travel is a necessity
& speed is a pleasure.

"How does this woman & her pirate get
into my dreams?" Yet I would have given
the world to please her if I only had the
chance. That moment decided my fate.

Ahead, the crowd separated aimlessly,
leaving an open path for the rioters.
Piracy, for him, was more about
changing the world than understanding it.

The great revolt of the colonies was not yet
in the air but serious looting began the next
day. It would seem that firms do not emerge
perfectly formed from the body of capitalism.

Captain Dampier makes notes about wild flowers

It is almost impossible to give any
sense of the violence of these storms,
yet we all know pirates who put off going
to the dentist for longer than they should.

He took me by the arm & dragged me
into the depths of the ship without any
regard for protocol. I would like to have
had a bath, a proper wallow with soap.

There is a kind of inevitability at work
here, yet the more mirrors there are,
the more glorious is the intimacy of the
room. The timing is clearly suspicious.

He's the total outlaw, a pure pirate,
yet he combines his grisly trade with
a passion for botany. The boys
surveyed all this then looked out to sea.

Abruptly there was a blinding flash as
the question of taxation began to raise
its ugly head. Social hot-spring bathing
is very much a part of pirate society.

One of the snakes had seized hold of its
own tail & the image whirled mockingly
before my eyes. "But I don't really like
chicken. I prefer manufactured meats".

Their relationship seemed to develop
as if life were imitating art, yet he was
interested in knowledge & its practical
application. Taxonomy rules, okay!

Once they had drunk of the elixir, the
pirates went off to build their sand castles.
They didn't know how to dance, so they
just stuck their hands in the air & waved.

As the mainstream of youth culture
floated downstream, the pirates paddled
against the flow. Their experimental
findings may not seem very surprising today.

It is to be hoped that he got what he deserved

A scene of despair dissolved into
a macabre kind of comedy as captain
Simpson issued orders from the quarter-
deck: "let's all go surfing today".

The human mind is a wonderfully
obtuse & circuitous instrument, yet to
make their grand statement, the
buccaneers had to reach for the moon.

Having hitched up his trousers, the old
tar sent forth a wondrous jet of tobacco
juice. When he wasn't busy with piracy
he spent his time recording animal sounds.

They had more of an intellectual
relationship than a love affair, yet
the external menace of the pirates
continued to feed their mutual attraction.

Actions, above all, deserve to be placed
in the front rank. How it had broken loose
was anyone's guess but he claimed her
as his flagship & took a dozen men captive.

The torchlight burned on their faces & their
bare shoulders & their skins were golden in
the glow. There are always some people who
dance & some who sit by the wall watching.

She was denounced as a drunk, a
promiscuous omnivore, a communist & finally,
as a pirate. The whole range of verbal wit is thus
made to serve the purpose of the dream work.

The futility of his position came to him with
a rush as the pirate paused, then moved
away. Soon every man on watch could see
the fire-ships bearing down on them.

Sex was in the air & this at a time when
more pirates than ever were doomed to
celibacy. His skin was a mass of scars,
a hideous covering of injured flesh.

Romeo & Ethel (the pirate's daughter)

She ate with an amazing appetite that
belied our preconceptions. Our whole
understanding of this angelic figure has
been replaced by a new respect.

He was a trader & a pirate too, yet the
pressure in all developed countries is
to send more & more people into higher
education. Piracy can also be marketed.

To my surprise, the portrait that emerged
was wholly lifelike. She paused to stretch
herself, her beautiful body uncoiling like a
snake, as Black Jack Davy breathed his last.

One could imagine a theoretical world
in which mutations were biased towards
improvement, yet the brains behind piracy
were the landed gentry of the far south west.

With her hectoring rhetoric, privet-hedge
propriety & thick hair piled into a steel
wave, she gained the air of a professional
dominatrix. Others managed to get more sleep.

The tribal elders ponder the meaning of life
away from the limits of the island, while the
pirate extracts the cork with infinite care &
pours each sailor a quarter glass of liquid.

In the split between 'the arties' & the 'social
realists', it has been argued that neither group
is right. Scouring the charity shops near the
homes of the rich & famous reveals fresh booty.

Typically, the pirates belonging to the enriched
group have a thicker brain cortex than those
outside this charmed circle. Our aim is to control
prices & also ration food & consumer essentials.

"Are you a book detective or a pirate?" Next to
join the frenzy are the clerks. On the other hand,
you could spend a lifetime researching the
physiology of walking, or just take to the high seas.

On the question of Pontius Pirate

Fortunately for us we live in a universe that
is at least partly comprehensible. The image
of the ship, so important to the legend of piracy,
has a long & celebrated history. Let it unwind.

I would cite the bravest as being those who were
the first to try chilli, lemon, lime, mustard, aniseed,
mushroom, onion, garlic & rhubarb. Nobody
wants to talk about rubbish—it's not sexy.

Hardly on dry land & the average buccaneer
develops a profound nostalgia for the briny.
He experiences a sort-of-reversal of sea-
sickness symptoms & a desire to walk the plank.

It has been said that at night, all cats seem
grey, but I prefer the one about the owl at
Minerva. The counterculture was less an
agent of chaos than a marginal commentary.

The above statement is open to discussion
yet this place suddenly smells strongly of
rotting Christmas trees. In the mythology of
seafaring, all bottles are recycled at leisure.

There was an increasing sense of chaos
yet the pirate scene had never been about
chaos. His streetwise oratory was vital in
convincing the volatile mob to set sail at all.

A strained creaking sound made him look up.
The corpse, already decayed & clothed with
gore, stood erect before the boy's eyes. This
was not singled out as a uniquely diabolical act.

Some pirates cultivate a reckless image while
others present a more dandified façade &
enjoy wearing good clothes. The knife
slipped & I saw it run deep into his finger.

He seemed remote from the others now,
though he acknowledged them often enough.
The water's surface grew calm again & the
whirlpools disappeared, one by one.

When the privateers returned from their pillage

"There needs to be fear & greed in the system in
order to make it tick". I could find no answer to this
statement & after a little persuasion agreed to become
one of the crew. "But I don't tell lies", I said, firmly.

A single seabird flapped upwards with a hoarse
cry as he entered the house of deep mourning.
The boom was feeding on itself & competition
was fierce for entry to the training school for pirates.

Nobody can say why you go chasing a pirate down
the street but such a state of affairs makes possible
a certain number of anxiety dreams. Was it the pirate,
you ask yourself, or was it the paranoia?

At what point does a civilisation hit its peak before it
declines, &, more germanely, how did a dish once as
humble as fish & chips become the preserve of the
affluent? Ginger Baker is sixty eight today.

By degrees, Nigel began to see himself as an avant-
gardist, yet each of the two interpretations has its
special meaning & leads us along different paths in
the dream analysis. Environments are never static.

Like the pirates, the sex pistols brought their own
entourage with them. There, for the first time, I met
teenagers who had trust funds instead of pocket
money. He was a man's man & liked throwing knives.

Choppy commodity markets gave the ruby stocks a
rough ride but this is not the time to let fear rule your
decisions. She was attractive, with humorous eyes,
black hair & well-rounded curves. Travel is a necessity.

Foul smells spread & disperse, one after the other, as
Johnny Pirate sweats profusely beneath his rubber
mask. Such a dynamic euphoria serves as an antithesis
to the static joys of family life, don't you agree?

His little ship lay snugly in a natural harbour well away
from the maelstrom, yet he seemed to be saying what
he had been made to say & nothing more. The best thing
to do is disengage. Roman Polanski is seventy four today.

The present was grim & the future looked worse

A hundred times during the day I felt the young man's
eyes upon me. The tentacles of the Octopus are sensitive
& can distinguish rough from smooth, heavy from light.

I do not remember how I got home, hours & hours later,
but sure enough there was the Jolly Roger, anchored in
the bay, the black flag of piracy flying from her mast.

Within the context of the time, he was saying the unsayable,
but suddenly, to say the unsayable was possible, even
desirable. I do not remember how I came to be at home.

I was the first to write & every day I gave my work to a young
woman to type up neatly. The soft sheen, the superb gilding,
not to mention the centuries of wisdom the books contained.

The pressure of population eased off & there followed a retreat
from the marginal lands. Sometimes the curse merged into
elaborate ritual magic. "He's a bloody pirate, a scallywag".

At the castle, the pirates were simply proving too strong.
Sheep, tolerant of humans to the point of boredom, moved
desultorily out of the way. Soon they were completely estranged.

The next thing I laid hold of was a brace of pistols & as I already
had a powder-horn & bullets I felt myself well supplied with arms.
I do not remember how I got home, hours & hours later.

Although we still retain a concept of memory in the deep,
collective sense, the new technologies change the nature of
the memorial process. I do not remember how I got home.

Treasure had transformed the Spanish Empire & heightened
its flaws. Now consider what happens when the bell rings just
before the food is presented. The summer enveloped us all.

The summer enveloped us all. In a country submerged in
nostalgia, this was a serious breach of etiquette. The illicit
part of me was now as voracious as my mouth had been.

Poor Poe, perennially broke & often drunk, seemed ideally
suited for the role.

One species of Charlock will supplant another

The pirate fleet, led by Caroline & London, acted as a focus for a separate
brand of discontent. A light in one of the cabins went on, then flicked off
again after a few moments. Stars, like individuals, age & change.

In myth & fairy tale, the metaphor of devouring often stands in for sex.
Rub shoulders with the third man & meet a very educated Rita, why doncha?
The counter culture soon came into contact with a culture of convenience.

He removes his mask with a flourish to reveal an eye patch (left) & a
monocle (right). The very term 'folk revival' implies that something
was already moribund. If you don't know where to stop, don't start!

It is widely believed that Birds' custard is one of the earliest examples
of convenience food. Improved methods of cultivation can increase our
supply so that we have no need to fear overpopulation in the future.

There were not many British seamen who missed the chance of piracy if
they saw it. We are undoubtedly in the realm of consumption. Production
in a modern economy generates uncertainty through time.

The masks gave people a liberty that turned the most refined ones into
hungry animals. This seems to say less about radio than about either tv
or film. All that remained was to take to the streets & tear down the walls.

Re-entry from peak experience is notoriously difficult to achieve yet the
sensations of sheep are not of unusual intensity. He was much thinner
than I'd remembered him, very pale & with a moist gleam about his face.

A culture of convenience is inevitably a culture of laziness. Yet something
within me was aware of an enormous gulf of darkness very close to us.
The same explanation which applies to phobias also applies to the anxiety
dream.

The hairiness of the beast has exercised great appeal in the literature of
piracy. It's strange how a random encounter in a foreign land can change
your whole life. However, let us not exaggerate our visual handicaps.

As piracy grew in complexity, rich influential men who enjoyed a gamble
took part in financing it. "We were all extremely ugly people. We were

outcasts, the unwashed". A sickness arose in me, more wretched than
anguish.

I began to recall what I knew of cannibals as the pirates worked out
a basic insurance scheme. I don't believe they knew that I was Long
John Silver.

Small arms to the quarter deck

She was more like a ship of the line but the anxiety we experience in dreams is only apparently explained by the dream content. Now think about the possibilities that might face a wingless male wasp.

Those who were in it for the money at the beginning now saw piracy as a form of fun. The moon was climbing higher & higher. The line between pirates & privateers is a thin one to modern eyes.

"How can you integrate something that is so life-shatteringly sublime with everyday existence without feeling cheated?" It was a hot afternoon & I can still remember the smell of honeysuckle all along the street.

Yet the musical analogy is a useful one. Since then the women had been meeting in secret whenever they were able. Their bodies shimmer in the light of the moon as they are borne up the beach on the crest of a wave.

Emotionally & creatively, they were at a virtual standstill. As the splash died away, a cheer of approval went up from those below deck. Now on these waves of the ebbing tide, the small fish began to reach our nets.

He was busy with a pirate boy who was dining at the desk on a silver platter of meats and fish. It's only when an ocean's swell eventually reaches shallow water that it starts to break. One could go further.

Only overwork is repulsive to human nature yet disgust seems to be one of the forces which have led to a restriction of the sexual aim. So the question is, why are insects so diverse?

The privateers would first meet over a bowl of rum punch on the captain's flagship overlooking the bay. This was probably the reason I avoided the beach where most of the village girls bathed.

The admiral then turned to an old pirate standby: ransom. This may be a form of habituation, but it is very long-lasting & can reasonably be regarded as a form of non-associative learning.

Since money would not buy anything, why sell something in order to get it? Treatment is more effective when accompanied by a certain degree of impressive ritual. The singers gave forth in front of the ship.

The moon was climbing higher & higher yet the musical analogy is a useful one. Piracy has existed since the earliest days of seafaring.

A shift in the earth's core

At the time of speaking the pirate economy is in dire straits.
He gave a deep sigh & then threw out his arms in agitated fashion.
All through the remainder of the afternoon, he was bored & restless.

It is not just the raging seas that concern a seaman. Let us
consider the relation of a drinker to his drink. This morning I gave
into the sudden fear that all this had been taking place in my head.

The pirates were wary of discussing their dreams, yet anyone who
has lived near tidal waters knows that the moon, far more than the
sun, controls the tides. In a sense, all human flesh is made of stardust.

He had another drink, scratched through his matted beard & dozed
again contentedly. The effects on the development of economic
power by the pirate can be shown in detail. Nothing is sacred.

It's hard to believe that this is a man who, in his younger
days, gained a reputation for wrecking hotel rooms & attacking
paparazzi. Storytelling can act as an agent of social bonding.

The truth of the matter is really fairly simple: the pirates were
resolute in defending their traditional rights. They understood
their desires & were already getting on with satisfying them.

Privateers are not essentially murderous, yet they can devastate
an area with a ruthless efficiency, reminiscent of a locust plague.
Somehow his gestures answered deeply to her need for warmth.

"Those pirates are playing at being bohemians", cried Spanker.
Yet the slim object, caught by the moon, became a thing of pure
dazzle, a shining pistol, highlighted in white & silver.

The buccaneer made it through the tempest only to face another
one when he arrived home. "Of all the cannibals on this island,
I have to get stuck with the craziest". His mood hit the doldrums.

Existing quietly in never-never land, the worker devotes his life to
producing objects which he does not own or control. British piracy
is alive & well & making a killing on tv & in Hollywood mythology.

The pirate assured me that his downfall began when he started to
listen to Barry Manilow. Alas, life is rarely so straightforward.

Criss-crossing the globe

In her encounter with the pirate, the female protagonist realises her match in more ways than one. The tide reaches flood stage, slackens, hesitates & begins to ebb. "Let's meet at the siren café".

Any man found plotting to leave the ship was immediately beheaded, yet political & moral coercion is giving way to freely adopted customs & norms. Pressure is a really good metaphor.

A dramatic change of pace came in the form of an excellent cover version of Brecht & Weill's *Pirate Jenny*. The legend of Blackbeard has inspired an impressive body of literature.

For a few minutes they steadied their legs, gazing out over the expanses of blue water. To the seventeenth century sailor, winds were animate creatures. The truth of the matter is simple.

If the pirates were rash enough to stay longer, they were killed or put into prison. His handsome face turns towards me as heroic optimism once more shades into gallows humour.

Already the moisture in his body was being leeched away by the sun as protest groups mushroomed at an alarming rate. With a taut sail she steers away as he clings there groaning on his rock.

The atmosphere in these lagoons is pretty enervating as the river narrows & mist rises from the surface of the water. The pirates are heading inshore to breed & they are arriving in vast numbers.

It was a masterpiece of cunning work. This time however, they were not to be deterred. When night fell some very strange creatures crept out of the crevices & crawled all over the reef.

Beautiful sirens live by the sea and lure unsuspecting sailors onto the rocks. The pirate ships, & later the pirate forts, held out for a further three years due to a mixture of cheek & legal loopholes.

They in turn attract visitors from the open ocean. Night came & with it an ebbing tide as they were torn to pieces by the teenage furies. It's best to start your own society & begin creating things for yourself.

The truth of the matter is never this simple yet punctuation is always, among other things, about   pausing.

Battle for priceless sunken treasure trove

A completely different possibility is the 'sit' & 'wait' solution, although it was long thought impossible that life of any sort could be found at such frozen depths. He breathed slowly, soothing them with the cool air.

Odysseus refuses to give the exact location of his latest find, yet there is only one other place in the world where this phenomenon has been observed. The patience of pirates is not equal to that of other men.

There are no controls on tourism in this area. As night falls, the group of brigands realise they are being stalked by a gigantic saltwater crocodile. A tremendous fight erupts & a breeze lightly brushes her skin.

Nobody had ever seen him so animated. The influence of the tides over the affairs of sea creatures has been well documented, but by the time he was sixteen, he was filled with self-loathing & incipient paranoia.

The pirate's death was filmed in slow motion as a single plastic bag fell from the edge of cliff & glided all the way down. I felt glad of the interruption, amazed that I'd started to talk about this stuff so quickly.

Tourist figures doubled in March upon the release of a film about a rogue 'saltie'. Now that the performance was over, those eyes had become inscrutable. The scent of roses was intense, like a drug.

The western Mediterranean is a graveyard of ships, sunk by pirates during Spain's long marine supremacy. A sign which fills one with consternation is the gradual disappearance of wood.

It began to rain, a steady, relentless drizzle. If the buccaneers don't get you then the saltwater crocodiles will. Various countries lay claim to colonial wrecks but we still feel safe in our anonymity.

Next to join the frenzy are the sharks, yet the grotto's waters teem with exotic marine life, including giant mussels, oversize sponges & luridly coloured coral. "A good man. Pirate! You look just like him".

The culture of piracy had gone mainstream. For the first time bohemia embraced fast-food. But the new dawn had scarcely touched the East with red before Odysseus put on his cloak & tunic.

As soon as the tide has ebbed, Convoluta rises from the sands of the forbidden zone.

& the parrot sat preening her plumage

A man who concentrates before a work of art is usually absorbed by it,
so how can any self-respecting buccaneer seriously consider wearing
leathers? He was the most magnificent animal I had ever seen.

The guards returned without their prisoners as the wind shifted abruptly
from west to south-west. Here we find eyes so simple that they barely
deserve to be recognised as eyes at all. Black Dog appears & disappears.

He was clad in city clothes & was probably the most elegant man I had
ever seen in my life. Occasionally, however, he abandons calm prophecy
for a rigorous exhortation to rebellion. A pirate's life was short, nasty &
      brutish.

From various directions, as the sound of the fog horns rang out in union, a
magnificent music echoed all over the harbour. A neighbouring fisherman
brings me the best of his catch, straight from the sea to my kitchen table.

After a while, I became possessed with the keenest curiosity about the nature
of the social whirl. The smoky blue eye-shadow emphasised her tiger-gold
eyes. All this excitement has led me to neglect my rationing system.

She had taken off her hat & veil & was standing before the large gold-framed
mirror, arranging her hair, when the door opened. It was not a learned
      pattern
of behaviour, it was a cat greeting a pirate. "Is this Ben Gunn a man",
      he asked?

& what had society done to throw a reasonable lady into such an excitement?
She looked dubious but followed my instructions & successfully managed
to do a basic move. It's been suggested that your pension is funding this
      genocide.

Only in the wilds of the Americas could he have flourished as he did, yet
anyone on the high seas took his chance, & piracy was as much an
accepted fact as any other danger. All these adventures were an open secret.

It was an exciting & powerful gesture yet here was another astonishing fact:
he loved working & was of an impatient temperament. The mythology of
wine can help us understand the usual ambiguity of our daily lives.

As Convoluta hit the bottle, the barking of a thousand dogs sounded in her ears. The saddest aspect of second-class piracy lies in self-hate & deprecation among the afflicted. She was doomed to a long career as a social misfit.

He led a hunted & sometimes desperate existence. A single buzzard circled the sky overhead but the landscape was empty & bleak.

The western capital of sin

They are waiting by the side of the sea. Three men are waiting
by the side of the sea. It is always the same three men & always
they wait. Within a local tradition innovation is unwelcome.

I often have the feeling that history is repeating itself yet I could
be completely wrong & have my theory blown out of the water.
In the meantime the breeze falls away & we become becalmed.

They are waiting by the side of the sea. Three men are waiting
by the side of the sea. It is always the same three men & always
they wait. Within a local tradition innovation is unwelcome.

As luck would have it a merchant ship was already under sail in
the harbour. Instantly, the figures reappeared, &, making a wide
circuit, prepared to head me off. It is always the same three men.

It is now impossible to imagine a life without worry yet fish
continue to leap from the water without the aid of enlarged
fins. Time passes yet everything stays the same. Or so it seems.

Allowing for time spent sleeping & on the essential task of eating,
not more than one hundred hours a week are available to the
buccaneer. It was not a good time to start examining taboos.

At other times the pirates became morose & morbid, regretting
the absence of meat & the weak taste of the wine. It is only the
time taken in shedding clothes that makes voyeurs of the public.

One man is wearing a green cloak. It is dark & shabby. He has
a hood & he is waiting like the others. The three men are spaced
at intervals of roughly twenty yards by the side of the sea.

For the second time I accompanied the pirate to the hospital &
we entered the house of the dead. No-one will ever know what
my feelings were at that moment but time passed just the same.

Naturally I needed to play to a full-house but the pirate wanted the
money in his back pocket, so we stopped for a break near the
trees. We both took the trouble to reload our weapons.

Like an enchantress who lures knights to her grotto, the
siren beckons. Yet it is always the same three men.

The object of their waiting becomes clear

Many of the pirates are masters of the grand style, yet their aim is
to break down cultural barriers, while attracting a wide audience.
Despite their efforts to exorcise the spectre of art, something lingers.

There were a number of passengers in the saloon & fifteen of these
were men. The loss of the boat had been discovered & pursuit would
begin in due course. "Not much mistake about that, Mr Spanker".

The pirate army pitched tent & settled in for the night. There was much
discussion about how to read in bed without getting cold in winter. The old
men shrugged their shoulders as the sexes drew further & further apart.

He had a hunted & sometimes desperate existence yet each of Morgan's
raids was remarkable for a different reason. Even after the restrictions
ended, the bed never became a symbol of the affluent society.

The sky was clear, the winds had abated & the full moon settled radiantly
in the dark. To keep her image fresh in the public's mind, Mary sent back
a letter from Port Royal. Her tastes leaned heavily towards the bizarre.

He continued to be astounded by the film's success, yet enclosed in the
floating stud-farms, the thoroughbreds are sheltered from all mongrel
marriages. It is an image that stays in the mind. I should say so.

Every stranger I meet in Hollywood is going to make my fortune. A cloud
passed across the sun & instantly the warmth was gone from the shelter
You need to rethink your fundamental principles & attempt to reapply them.

A little further back, there was a kind of grotto where the palm & banana
trees crowded so thickly, they blocked out the sun. The greatest power the
world has ever seen can march into a country & demand regime change.

As the darkness & cold deepened, I saw the pirate captain waving to her
from the portico. It was an unexpected & exciting gesture yet Mary wasn't
interested. He turned away to talk to somebody else.

Had it been Silver & his lads creeping in on them not a soul would have
made daybreak, but I'd never seen such spontaneous warmth expressed by
pirates. It was humiliating. Had their brains been invaded by alien parasites?

Democracy, the dominant political myth of our time is founded upon the
notion of piracy. The present is grim & the future looks worse.

The Empire of Fear

For a moment the light disappeared
behind the rise of a dune. How far do
ants help in allowing us to think through
what we are doing? Here the lexicon
of advertising is telling. By happy
coincidence, the Dayglo Pirate was
already planning his departure. A
hobby is the happy medium between
a passion & a monomania & many a
pirate was a gleeful monomaniac!
It is apparently always difficult to
leave a voluntary organisation yet
these people have a great deal of
money. If the pirates were radical
democrats, then the Spanish were
monarchists.

All roads surely lead to Rome yet it
might be nice to spend a few days in
Venice. A certain puritanical captain
had long sensed moral danger in
credit but the pirates went fishing
for their favourite food, the lump-
sucker. Current thinking believes them
to be poisonous, but If you think
education is expensive perhaps you
should try ignorance. His fear of attack
overwhelmed common sense, yet hermit
crabs, swimming crabs & sand-hoppers
were also devoured. Pirates spend
most of their lives at sea but each year
for just a few weeks they have to return
to the coast in order to breed.

I noticed two men in dark red uniforms,
carrying muskets, standing at the back
of the crowd. For the next year we could
all throw ourselves into the crusade with

gusto. Here we have the elements of a
rich, strategic game. A curious shipwreck
left him trembling in terror but they taught
him breathing techniques & the arts of
embellishment. Instantly the light cleared
& he was too astonished to even touch
the gun. By a coincidence, they were both
dressed in white yet we were unable to
make any impression & the juice of the
language is missing. Here we have the
elements of a rich, strategic game.

On the upper decks, the dangers came
from musketry, stray cannon shot &
falling masts & spars. To lose control
of one's limbs is a problem hard to
ignore, yet he was a pessimist, whereas
almost all of the others are in some
sense, optimists. An influx from the
cities not only changed the lives of the
buccaneers but ensured that the press-
gangs pressed even harder. Then began
one of those nightmare voyages the sea
sometimes imposes. Those pirates who
were known to have vivid dreams felt
themselves to be growing fins in place of
limbs. The examiners had certainly
done their homework. When land
animals return to the water, why don't
they rediscover the full apparatus of
watery living?

A vast cloud of dark smoke began
to rise from the harbour as Captain
Swing made his first foray away
from dry land. He was the idol of
his followers. Looking up, he could
see some of the stars, a sickle-moon
& the clouds scudding by on the

wind. There is a profound suspicion
of intellectuals to start with, yet I
can't get the image of a young
child playing a bassoon to an
earthworm, out of my head. It was
not exactly an offensive act but such
a scene of despair dissolved into
a macabre kind of comedy. By an
unhappy coincidence, the Captain
was already planning his departure,
when a strained creaking sound
made him look up. It was the last
recorded incident of the voyage.

Whenever he stopped, we would
exchange ideas with the utmost
seriousness. These were repeated
over & over by musicians scattered
around the room. As a debunking
exercise, this had much to offer,
but it overbalanced into strained
hysteria. I was acutely conscious
of the flood of eroticism which
seethed all around me, yet we
take our technological world, &
our memories within it, very much
for granted. Pirates can suffer high
levels of stress in environments
where alcohol & drugs are
widely available.

For most of her adult life, she had
been aware of popular protest,
even feeling instinctive sympathy
for it. Once liberated, unchained &
in revolt, sexuality becomes man's
mortal enemy: discuss. In the distance,
he heard the muted splashing of water,
yet a whole psychodrama is quickly

enacted when an image is interpreted.
The Barbary Corsairs' mixture of Norse
square sails & Arab sails, enabled pirates
to get closer to their victims before
swiftly outrunning the naval ships sent
to pursue them. Well, perhaps such
things are best left as treasured
memories! His literary tastes were
becoming more political & prosaic.
At the castle, the pirates were simply
proving too strong, while he was in
France, without papers, risking arrest.

In moments of acute emotion the
human brain plays strange tricks.
What members we lost to the cult
were probably soon regained, yet
the panic came upon me again in
full blast. On his upper decks, he
had hundreds of men with muskets,
bayonets, cutlasses, pistols & hand-
grenades. Every time I remember
these events, I recreate a memory
anew. Why not build a nest? Many
pirates have highly-developed
sebaceous glands, yet their
personal hygiene is often lacking.
Such openness provides a further
level of indeterminacy to the
functioning of both brain & behaviour.
People understood what he meant,
even though he managed to mangle it
as he said it.

A sharp shock was required
to get a reaction from dulled
reflexes as the sound of
shuffling feet awoke him.
She whispered to him & he

smiled, not understanding
the words but knowing their
meaning. "It isn't only pirates
that have memories". At first
sight this might be seen as
encouraging but everything
pales before the demand of
the instant. Promiscuity or
saturation occur as reactions
to scarcity. This sounds
like something he might
have learned at pirate
school!

The thing 'the pirates' liked
about 'the ants' is that they
worked so very hard. Since
few people knew each other,
nobody really knew what to
talk about. She hears stories
in her head & they are like
dreams being recited by
somebody else. Reading
philosophy, he discovered,
produces a strange 'drunkenness',
entirely unlike anything else.
There is a reported case of
a pirate cutting a man to
pieces & then licking
the blade clean.

Primary Sources

The Coral Island, R.M. Ballantyne; *The Drowned World* & *The Complete Short Stories*, J.G. Ballard; *Mythologies*, Roland Barthes; *The System of Objects*, Jean Baudrillard; *The Pirates of the Spanish Main*, Douglas Botting; *The Faber Book of Science*, ed. John Carey; *Alice in Wonderland*, Lewis Carroll; *The Bloody Chamber* & *American Ghosts* & *Old World Wonders*, Angela Carter; *The Pursuit of the Millennium*, Norman Cohn; *Altered States—The Story of Ecstasy Culture* & *Acid House*, Matthew Collins; *The Penguin Book of Horror Stories*, ed. A.J. Cuddon; *The Origin of Species*, Charles Darwin; *Indian Vegetarian Curries*, Harvey Day; *Climbing Mount Improbable*, Richard Dawkins; *A General History of the Pirates*, Daniel Defoe; *Robinson Crusoe*, Daniel Defoe; *When the Music's Over*, Robin Denselow; *The Libertine*, dir. Laurence Dunmore; *The Buccaneers of America*, John Esquemeling; *The Interpretation of Dreams* & *Jokes* & *their Relation to the Unconscious*, Sigmund Freud; *The World Economy since the Wars*, J.K. Galbraith; *In Search of the Buccaneers*, Anthony Gambrill; *Dinosaurs in a Haystack—Selections in Natural History*, S.J. Gould; *Smoke Signals*, ed. Lavinia Greenlaw; *The Blue Planet*, dir. Steve Greenwood; *Steppenwolf*, Herman Hesse; *Slow Death*, Stewart Home; *The Odyssey*, Homer; *The Making of the English Landscape*, W.G. Hoskins; *British Sea Power—How Britain became Sovereign of the Seas*, David Howarth; *The State We're In*, Will Hutton; *Best New Erotica*, ed. Maxim Jakubowski; *Lost Hearts*, MR James; *The History of Rasselas*, Samuel Johnson; *The Single Helix—A Turn Around the World of Science*, Steve Jones; *No Logo*, Naomi Klein; *The Case of Charles Dexter Ward*, H.P. Lovecraft; *Revolution in the Head—The Beatles' Records* & *the Sixties*, Ian MacDonald; *The Communist Manifesto*, Karl Marx & Friedrich Engels; *No Pockets in a Shroud*, Horace McCoy; *Revolt into Style—The Pop Arts in the Fifties* & *Sixties*, George Melly; *Moby Dick*, Herman Melville; *The Pirate*, dir. Vincente Minnelli; *Delta of Venus—Erotica*, Anaïs Nin; *The Death of Economics*, Paul Ormerod; *The Black Pirate*, dir. Albert Parker; *Pirates*, L. Du Garde Peach; *Pirates*, David Pickering; *Selected Tales*, Edgar Allan Poe; *The Ninth Gate*, dir. Roman Polanski; *Pirates*, dir. Roman Polanski; *The Third Man*, dir. Carol Reed; *Interview with the Vampire*, Anne Rice; *Sonic Harvest—Towards Musical Democracy*, Sam Richards; *The Making of Memory*, Steven Rose; *England's Dreaming—The Sex Pistols* & *Punk Rock*, John Savage; *Treasure Island*, R.L. Stevenson; *Dracula*, Bram Stoker; *Empire of Blue Water—Henry Morgan* & *the Pirates who Ruled the Caribbean Waves*, Stephen Talty; *Religion* & *the Decline of Magic*, Keith Thomas; *The Making of the English Working Class*, E.P. Thompson; *Ocean of Sound*, David Toop; *Helen* & *Desire*, Alexander Trocchi; *Tom Sawyer*, Mark Twain; *From the Beast to the Blond—On Fairy Tales* & *their Tellers*, Marina Warner; *Pirates of the Caribbean—The Curse of the Black Pearl*, dir. Gore Verbinski; *Waterhouse on Newspaper Style*, Keith Waterhouse; *Citizen Kane*, dir. Orson Welles; *Karl Marx*, Francis Wheen; *Sea Fishing for Beginners*, Maurice Wiggin; *Double Indemnity*, dir. Billy Wilder; *The Passion*, Jeanette Winterson; *Orlando*, Virginia Woolf.

Lightning Source UK Ltd.
Milton Keynes UK
11 August 2010

158204UK00002B/5/P

9 781848 610972